# The Senses

**Rufus Bellamy**

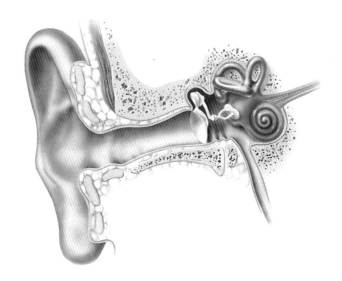

W

FRANKLIN WATTS

LONDON•SYDNEY

First published in 2004 by Franklin Watts
96 Leonard Street, London EC2A 4XD

Franklin Watts Australia
45–51 Huntley Street
Alexandria, NSW 2015

Series editor: Adrian Cole
Series design: White Design
Art director: Jonathan Hair
Picture research: Diana Morris
Educational consultant: Beverley Goodger
Medical consultant: Dr Gabrielle Murphy

A CIP catalogue record for this book is available from the British Library.

ISBN: 0 7496 5143 1

Printed in Malaysia

Acknowledgements:
Special thanks to our model Imani Jawarah

Bettmann/Corbis: 11b. Mark Clarke/
SPL: 23b. Colin Cuthbert/SPL: 15b.
Chris Fairclough: 13b, 25b
Paul Hardy/Corbis: 11c.
James King-Holmes/SPL: 21b.
P. Kaplan/Art Directors & Trip:
front cover, 5. Rory McClenaghan/
SPL: 26b. Ray Moller: 23t Prof.
P. Motta/ Dept. of Anatomy/
University 'La Sapienza', Rome/SPL: 10b,
19b, 26t. Alfred Pasieka/SPL: 29b.
Ken Powell/Trip: 9b.
Dale C. Spartas/
Corbis: 17b. SPL: 8tr.

# Contents

# The senses are our
# gateway to the world

**W**e know about the world because we can see, hear, touch, smell and taste. These five senses are the gateway through which we experience everything that happens around us.

The eyes, ears, skin, nose and tongue are the sense organs that detect what is happening outside the body. They change sensory information into electrical nerve impulses, which are then sent to the brain. The brain processes these nerve impulses and we experience them as sensations, for example sights, sounds and tastes.

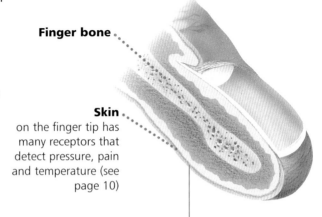

**Finger bone**

**Skin**
on the finger tip has many receptors that detect pressure, pain and temperature (see page 10)

### Sense of touch

*The fingers and hands are one of the most sensitive areas of the skin (see page 11).*

### Sense of taste

*The surface of the tongue is covered with taste receptors that can detect sweet, sour, salty and bitter flavours (see page 14).*

### The sense organs

All sense organs contain special receptor cells that respond to different things. For example, receptors in the eyes respond to light, those in the ears respond to sound, those in the skin respond to lots of different kinds of touch, those in the nose respond to odour molecules in the air and those in the tongue respond to taste chemicals in food. The things that the sense organs respond to are called stimuli.

### Senses of smell and hearing

*The nose provides information about the hidden world of scents (see page 16). The ears help us to communicate, to keep out of danger and to even discover where some things are (see pages 18–21).*

## Sense of sight

*The eyes contain light receptors that let us see the world around us (see page 24).*

## The importance of senses

Senses are vital. The senses help keep us safe, let us enjoy life and enable us to learn things. Without them, we would not avoid a hot fire or enjoy eating a cold ice cream. Our senses also provide us with the experiences that we learn from and remember – our memories. Our senses help make us who we are.

## Valuing our senses

It is important not to take the senses for granted. Many people live their lives with one or more of their senses damaged and have to overcome the problems that this causes.

## Roller coaster thrills

*Funfair rides provide lots of thrills because they overstimulate some sense organ receptor cells.*

## ONLY FIVE SENSES?

Sight, hearing, touch, smell and taste are the five main senses. But many different receptors inside the body can also 'sense' things, such as how hot the body is, movement and how thirsty we are. We are not as aware of this internal sensory system as we are of the five senses, but it is just as important – without it the body would stop working properly.

# Information from the sense organs
# is sent to the brain

The brain receives information from the sense organs in the form of nerve impulses. The brain analyses these impulses and compares them to stored sensory information to understand what is happening in the world around us.

**Sensing victory**
*These fans cheer after seeing their team score a goal.*

**Cerebrum**
largest part of the brain

**Temporal lobe**
receives and analyses impulses from the ears

**Frontal lobe**
controls movements, speech and thought

**Parietal lobe**
receives impulses from touch and pain receptors

**Occipital lobe (visual cortex)**
receives and analyses impulses from the eyes

**Cerebral cortex**
the bumpy surface layer of the cerebrum where nerve impulses are sent

**Cerebellum**
helps control movement and balance

## Getting the message

When the impulses from the sense organs reach the brain, they go to different areas of the brain's surface. This layer is called the cerebral cortex and looks like the bumpy, folded surface of a cauliflower. Areas in the middle and side of the cerebral cortex (see above) receive impulses about touch, taste, hearing and smell. Nerve impulses from the eyes go to an area at the back of the brain called the occipital lobe (visual cortex).

**Brain stem**
connected to the spinal cord

### The human brain (left side)

*We know if something tastes nice, feels hot or smells sweet because different parts of the brain tell us.*

6

## Understanding sensations

Sensory information is processed in the brain to become sensations. For example, we describe some sensations as: 'bumpy', 'sweet', 'loud', 'stinky' and 'dark'. This happens on the left and right sides of the brain in the cerebral cortex. To understand what is happening, the brain compares new impulses to information it has already stored through previous experiences. This process begins at a young age when we first begin to recognise things, such as what food flavours we like and what different sounds mean.

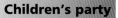

**Children's party**

*We begin to understand different combinations of sensory information at a young age. For example, these children are choosing food to eat based on colour, texture, smell and finally taste.*

## HOT OR COLD?

Conduct this experiment to see how the brain can be tricked by the information it gets from the sense organs. Ask an adult to fill three glasses with cold, warm and hot water (ask the adult to check that the water is not too hot to touch). Now cool one of your fingers in the cold water and heat another finger in the hot water.

After a while, dip your cold and hot fingers one at a time into the warm water. You should find that the warm water feels hot to your cold finger and cold to your hot finger. This happens because your skin sends information to your brain about temperature differences, not actual temperatures.

**Mixed messages**

*Try this experiment and you will see that your senses can play tricks on your brain.*

# The nervous system
# carries nerve impulses

The sense organs send impulses to the brain along nerves. Nerves connect almost every part of the body to the brain. Nerve impulses from the ears, nose, mouth and eyes travel along specific nerves straight to the brain. Nerve impulses from most touch receptors travel from the skin to the brain along nerves that pass up the spinal cord.

**Nerves**

*Nerves like these carry nerve impulses all over the body.*

### Nerves

Nerves are made up of bundles of special cells called neurons. These are very long cells – the longest can be around one metre long. There are three types of neurons: sensory neurons carry nerve impulses from the sense organs to the brain and spinal cord. Motor neurons carry nerve impulses from the brain and spinal cord back to the muscles. Association neurons carry nerve impulses between neurons in the brain and the spinal cord.

**Brain**
receives impulses from the sense organs, analyses them and responds

**Association neuron**
carry impulses between other neurons in the brain and spinal cord

**Sensory neuron**
carries impulses from the sense organ

**Motor neuron**
carries impulses to the muscle fibres

**Spinal cord**
carries impulses between the brain and other parts of the body

### The nervous system

*The nervous system connects different parts of the body to the brain, like the wires of a telephone network.*

### Nerve impulse pathway

*Sensory neurons carry nerve impulses to the brain via the spinal cord. The brain responds by sending new impulses along the spinal cord to motor neurons which enter the muscles.*

## Nerve impulses

When the receptor at the end of a sensory neuron gets a strong enough stimulation, impulses travel towards the brain along the nerve. Nerve impulses can only travel in one direction along a neuron.

## Brain response

Once the brain receives sensory nerve impulses, it analyses them and reacts. For example, if something tastes nasty the brain may instruct the muscles in the mouth to spit the food out. To move a group of muscles the brain sends out new nerve impulses. These travel down motor neurons. When they get to a muscle, the impulses cause a chemical reaction that makes the muscle contract.

**1. Touch receptor**
in the skin is stimulated and sends a nerve impulse

**Direction of nerve impulse**

**Nerve fibre**

**2. Association neuron**
passes the nerve impulse up the spinal cord to the brain

**A sensory neuron**

*Nerve impulses run from receptors in the skin along a sensory neuron to an association neuron in the spinal cord.*

## NERVE FIBRE SPEED

Different types of sensory impulses travel at different speeds along different types of nerve. You can feel this in action if you stub your toe. You will first feel the touch of your toe on the ground, because this type of sensation is carried in fast nerve fibres. A split second later, you'll feel pain, since pain is carried by slower fibres.

### Speedy impulses

*Impulses in the slowest nerve fibres travel at walking speed. Some nerve fibres, such as those carrying impulses from this motorcyclist's muscles, travel at over 300 km/h. That's faster than his motorbike!*

# Touch receptors send
# information to the brain

When we touch or hold something, we get a lot of information about it, for example whether it is hot or cold, smooth or rough. Skin contains many different types of receptor that send this information to the brain. Each type responds to a different sort of stimulus, including pressure, vibration, temperature and pain. Together, they give the brain a full sensory 'description' of what is touching the skin.

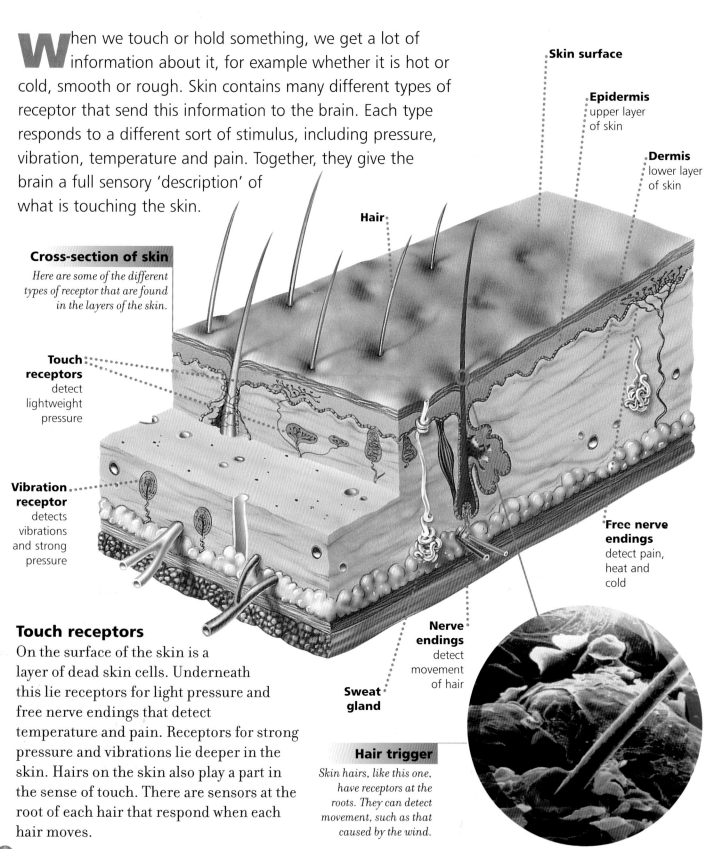

**Skin surface**

**Epidermis**
upper layer
of skin

**Dermis**
lower layer
of skin

**Hair**

**Cross-section of skin**
*Here are some of the different
types of receptor that are found
in the layers of the skin.*

**Touch
receptors**
detect
lightweight
pressure

**Vibration
receptor**
detects
vibrations
and strong
pressure

**Free nerve
endings**
detect pain,
heat and
cold

**Nerve
endings**
detect
movement
of hair

**Sweat
gland**

## Touch receptors
On the surface of the skin is a layer of dead skin cells. Underneath this lie receptors for light pressure and free nerve endings that detect temperature and pain. Receptors for strong pressure and vibrations lie deeper in the skin. Hairs on the skin also play a part in the sense of touch. There are sensors at the root of each hair that respond when each hair moves.

### Hair trigger
*Skin hairs, like this one,
have receptors at the
roots. They can detect
movement, such as that
caused by the wind.*

## Sensitivity

Some parts of the body have more touch sensors than others – for example, the pads of the fingers have a lot of light pressure touch sensors. This is why they are so sensitive. The illustration (right) shows the touch sensitivity of some parts of the body.

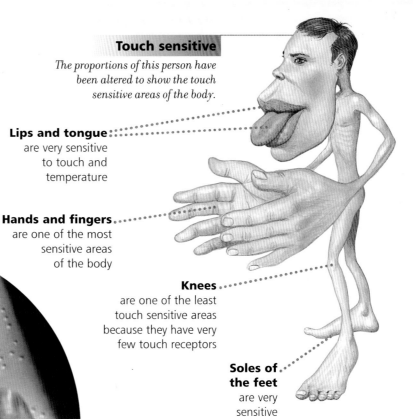

*The proportions of this person have been altered to show the touch sensitive areas of the body.*

**Lips and tongue**
are very sensitive to touch and temperature

**Hands and fingers**
are one of the most sensitive areas of the body

**Knees**
are one of the least touch sensitive areas because they have very few touch receptors

**Soles of the feet**
are very sensitive

## Reading by touch

The sense of touch is very important for people who have lost the sense of sight and are blind. They can use their highly-developed sense of touch to read with their finger tips by using Braille – a special type of alphabet made up of raised dots.

## LOUIS BRAILLE (1809–52)

Braille was invented in France in 1829 by a man called Louis Braille (right). He was only three years old when he lost his sight after injuring his eyes. He invented his system to give blind people an easy-to-use way to read and learn. The Braille system uses six dots arranged in a rectangular 'cell'. Single dots or combinations of dots represent the different letters of the alphabet. For example, the letter 'a' is represented by a single dot.

Today, many books are printed in Braille. Watches, playing cards and computer keyboards have been designed featuring Braille lettering.

# Pain is part of
# the sense of touch

**W**hen we touch something that is very hot, we feel pain, and this makes us move away from the heat (the source of the pain) very quickly. This is why pain is an important part of the sense of touch. It protects us from danger, for example it stops us being seriously burned.

## What is pain?

Pain occurs when the body is injured or experiences extreme stimuli – for example, crushing pressure. This is detected by pain receptors: free nerve endings that are found in the skin and elsewhere in the body, such as inside the teeth.

**Source of pain**

4.

2.

1.

3.

### Reflex action

*1. Free nerve endings sense pain in the hand.*
*2. Nerve impulses from the sense receptors travel to the spinal cord and straight to the arm muscles.*
*3. Muscles receive the nerve impulses and pull the arm away from the source of pain.*
*4. Nerve impulses arrive at the brain and we feel pain, but the hand has already moved.*

**Spinal cord**

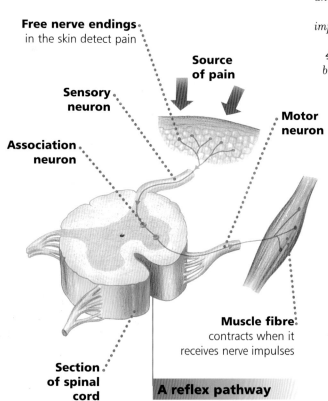

**Free nerve endings**
in the skin detect pain

**Source of pain**

**Sensory neuron**

**Motor neuron**

**Association neuron**

**Muscle fibre**
contracts when it receives nerve impulses

**Section of spinal cord**

### A reflex pathway

*This is how a nerve impulse takes a short cut to create a reflex action.*

## Reflexes

Pain often makes us react very quickly. This happens because the nerve impulses from the pain receptors are 'short-circuited' when they get to the spinal cord. Instead of going to the brain, they are sent straight to whichever muscles must act to stop the body being injured. This is called a reflex action. Nerve impulses reach the brain to tell it what has happened only after movement has started.

## AMAZING SKIN

Skin is the main organ of touch (in fact, it is the body's largest organ) but it has many other uses. It keeps you dry and protects you from germs that might cause illness. It also helps to keep your body at the correct temperature. One of the body's internal sensors (inside a part of the brain called the hypothalamus) monitors your temperature. If you get too hot, the hypothalamus sends out messages that activate sweat glands in the skin. When sweat evaporates from the skin it takes heat away from the body and cools it down.

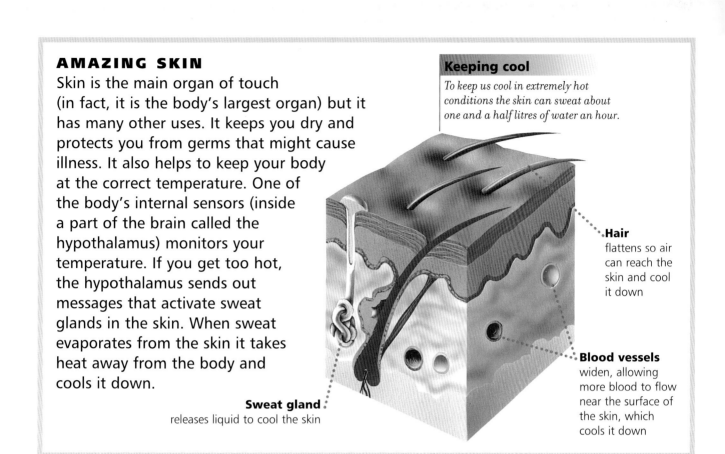

**Keeping cool**

*To keep us cool in extremely hot conditions the skin can sweat about one and a half litres of water an hour.*

**Hair**
flattens so air can reach the skin and cool it down

**Blood vessels**
widen, allowing more blood to flow near the surface of the skin, which cools it down

**Sweat gland**
releases liquid to cool the skin

## The importance of pain

Pain is very important, not only because it prevents serious injuries, but also because it tells us to rest when we put the body under too much stress. Pain is a very strong 'learning experience' – if we hurt ourselves, we try not to make the same mistake again in the future.

**Feeling ill**

*When we are ill, pain also helps doctors understand what is wrong with us.*

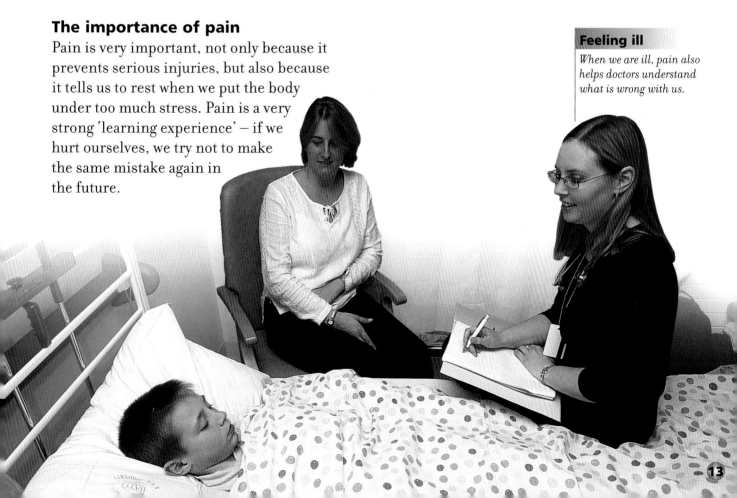

# The taste receptors detect
# **different flavours**

**W**ithout the sense of taste we would not be able to enjoy eating and drinking. Taste also helps to stop us eating bad or poisonous food. We sense taste because receptors in the tongue respond to molecules in food. When we eat, food is partly dissolved by saliva in the mouth. This causes the food to release the molecules we can taste. These molecules stimulate the tongue's sense receptors, contained inside the taste buds, to send nerve impulses to the brain.

**Taste bud**

*Each papilla contains taste buds like this one. Each taste bud contains taste receptors. Practise copying and labelling diagrams by tracing this illustration.*

**Outer layer of the papilla**

**Nerve fibres**
carry nerve impulses to the brain

**Papilla (cross section)**
forms a tiny bump on the tongue's surface and contains taste buds

**Taste pore**
taste molecules stimulate the taste bud here

**Taste receptor cell**
sends nerve impulses to the brain

**Bitter**
flavours are detected at the back

**Taste map**

*The surface of the tongue contains thousands of papillae arranged in a special way. Certain parts of the tongue are sensitive to each of the four main tastes: sweet, salty, sour or bitter.*

**Sour**
flavours are detected at the sides

## Taste buds

The tongue has a rough surface (use a mirror to look at your tongue). This is caused by thousands of tiny bumps called papillae. On the side of each of these are taste buds that contain taste sense receptors. There are four types of taste bud. Each bud responds most strongly to one specific taste molecule: sweet, salty, sour or bitter. The four types of taste bud are located in different areas of the tongue: sweet at the front, salty at the front and sides, sour at the sides and bitter at the back.

**Sweet**
flavours are detected at the front

**Salty**
flavours are detected at the front and sides

## Flavours

All the different flavours we taste are combinations of the four main tastes. We can taste many different flavours because the brain combines the information it gets from the different taste buds.

## That looks and smells tasty

The sense of taste does not work alone. The sensations we experience when we eat are produced by a combination of information from the taste and smell receptors. In fact, smell is much more sensitive than taste.

Sight also plays a part. When we look at food we can often tell if it is good or bad, for example we would not eat a mouldy apple.

**Eyes**
provide information about how food looks

**Nose**
receptors provide information on how food smells

**Tongue**
receptors detect taste, touch, temperature and pain

### Combination of senses

*When we eat we receive a combination of nerve impulses from sense receptors in the taste buds, nose and eyes. These provide us with information about the food that is analysed in the brain.*

## ARTIFICIAL FLAVOURS

Many snack foods and sweets contain artificial flavours. Scientists make these by extracting the molecules that make up a particular flavour from the actual food itself. They analyse these molecules using machines that can tell them exactly what chemicals are present. These chemicals are then created artificially and added to foods such as potato crisps and sweets.

### Flavour improvement

*Scientists are always trying to improve the taste of artificial flavours. This scientist is carrying out flavour research. She is injecting chemicals into a tomato before she blends it in the machine. The results from the test will help to produce a new 'improved' tomato flavour.*

# The nose senses
# odour molecules in the air

Whether detecting the scent of a flower or the stink of a blocked drain, the nose lets us experience the hidden world of smells. Things smell because they contain odour molecules that can easily float away into the air. Receptors inside the nose respond to these odour molecules. Things that do not contain these molecules – like a bit of glass – do not smell.

Smell is an incredibly sensitive and mysterious sense – scientists still know little about how it actually works.

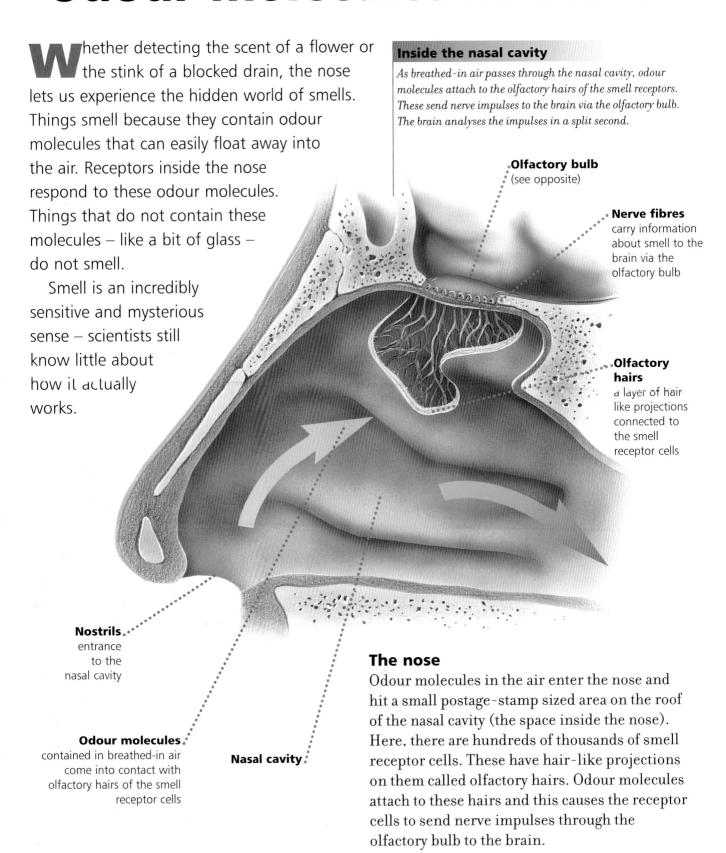

### Inside the nasal cavity

*As breathed-in air passes through the nasal cavity, odour molecules attach to the olfactory hairs of the smell receptors. These send nerve impulses to the brain via the olfactory bulb. The brain analyses the impulses in a split second.*

**Olfactory bulb**
(see opposite)

**Nerve fibres**
carry information about smell to the brain via the olfactory bulb

**Olfactory hairs**
a layer of hair like projections connected to the smell receptor cells

**Nostrils**
entrance to the nasal cavity

**Odour molecules**
contained in breathed-in air come into contact with olfactory hairs of the smell receptor cells

**Nasal cavity**

### The nose

Odour molecules in the air enter the nose and hit a small postage-stamp sized area on the roof of the nasal cavity (the space inside the nose). Here, there are hundreds of thousands of smell receptor cells. These have hair-like projections on them called olfactory hairs. Odour molecules attach to these hairs and this causes the receptor cells to send nerve impulses through the olfactory bulb to the brain.

## Smelling

Scientists think that there could be hundreds of different types of smell receptor cell, each one capable of distinguishing a different type of odour molecule. Because of this we can tell the difference between about 10,000 different smells.

Smell plays a vital part in allowing us to experience different flavours when we eat. A blocked nose, for example as a result of a cold, reduces the sense of taste.

**Nerve fibres**
carry information about smell via the olfactory bulb to the brain

**Smell receptor cells**
send information about smell to the olfactory bulb

## Smell and feelings

The nerve impulses from the smell receptor cells travel along nerves through the roof of the nose to the olfactory bulb. They then go through parts of the brain that store memories and produce emotions. That is why smells can make us feel strong emotions and bring back vivid memories.

### Olfactory bulb
*All the smell receptor nerve fibres meet in the olfactory bulb. It is an 'extension' of the brain.*

### Smell patrol
*Some dogs, such as this one, have a highly-developed sense of smell. They can be trained to search for things, such as illegal drugs.*

## GOOD SNIFFERS

Many animals can see, feel, hear and taste much better than human beings. The same is true for the sense of smell. Some animals specialise in smelling certain scents that are important to the way they live. For example, a male silkworm moth can sense the smell of a female silkworm moth over ten kilometres away. Sharks also have an amazing sense of smell. Most sharks can detect scent in tiny quantities when they hunt for prey. In fact, a great white shark could smell a single drop of blood in an Olympic-sized swimming pool.

# Sound waves travel through
# the air into the ears

**W**e use our sense of hearing to help us communicate, to keep out of danger and even to discover where some things are. Sounds are produced when things vibrate – for example, a guitar's plucked string – and disturb the air, creating sound waves.

## Sound waves

Sound waves spread out through the air from the source of the sound. We can hear because the ears convert sound waves into electrical nerve impulses that can be analysed by the brain.

**Plucking strings**

*All musical instruments produce sound waves. When a musician plays different notes he or she produces different shaped sound waves.*

## SOUND WAVE PRODUCTION

When you listen to a radio your ears pick up the sound waves produced by the speaker in the radio. Speakers work because they convert the electrical signal they receive into forwards and backwards movement of the cone inside them. This makes the air around the speaker move and forms sound waves. Look carefully at the cone of a large speaker when it is playing; you should see it moving.

**Listening to music**

*The sound waves from this girl's headphones are turned into electrical impulses in her inner ear. Be careful when using headphones – sounds that are too loud can permanently damage hearing.*

## The outer and middle ear

The earflaps (or pinnae) funnel sound waves down the ear canal. The ear canal leads to the rest of the ear that is protected inside the skull. At the end of the ear canal is a very thin membrane called the eardrum. When sound waves hit the eardrum it vibrates. In the middle ear three small bones (the smallest ones in the body) pass this vibration to a piece of flexible tissue called the oval window, which sits at the entrance to the inner ear.

## The inner ear

The inner ear is where the vibrations caused by sounds are converted into electrical impulses, which are sent to the brain. This happens in the cochlea, an extremely complicated structure that is shaped like a snail's shell. It is made up of three fluid-filled tubes that are coiled up together and separated by very thin membranes.

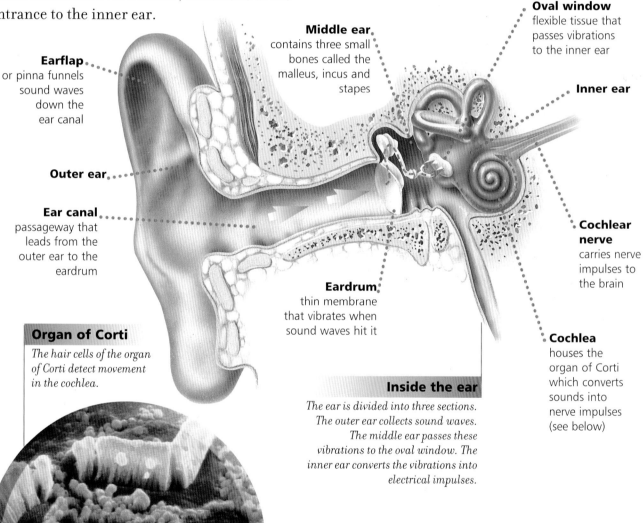

**Earflap**
or pinna funnels sound waves down the ear canal

**Outer ear**

**Ear canal**
passageway that leads from the outer ear to the eardrum

**Middle ear**
contains three small bones called the malleus, incus and stapes

**Eardrum**
thin membrane that vibrates when sound waves hit it

**Oval window**
flexible tissue that passes vibrations to the inner ear

**Inner ear**

**Cochlear nerve**
carries nerve impulses to the brain

**Cochlea**
houses the organ of Corti which converts sounds into nerve impulses (see below)

**Organ of Corti**

*The hair cells of the organ of Corti detect movement in the cochlea.*

**Inside the ear**

*The ear is divided into three sections. The outer ear collects sound waves. The middle ear passes these vibrations to the oval window. The inner ear converts the vibrations into electrical impulses.*

## Making nerve impulses

When the oval window vibrates, it produces movements in the fluid and membranes of the cochlea. These movements are detected by hair cells that line the narrow central tube in the cochlea (the organ of Corti). The hair cells then send electrical nerve impulses to the brain, which analyses them and interprets them as sounds.

# The ears send nerve impulses
## to the brain

The brain has an amazing ability to distinguish between an almost limitless number of different sounds. For example, we can listen to a pop group and tell the difference between all the instruments and the notes they play. We can do this because the ears provide the brain with lots of information about the sound waves they pick up. The ear can also hear a tremendous range of sounds – the loudest noise we can stand is about ten million, million times the power of the quietest sound we can detect.

**Wave air pressure**

*Every sound we hear is caused by sound waves that move air backwards and forwards. The peaks of the wave are the places where the air has been squashed together. The troughs are the places where the air has been spread out.*

**Frequency**
the number of complete waves produced every second is linked to the pitch of the sound – the more waves per second the higher the pitch

**Amplitude**
the height of the wave shows the volume of that part of the sound – the higher the waves are, the louder the sound

**Trough**

**Peak**

**Pitch and frequency**

Different sounds make the air move in different ways. For example, a high-pitched sound has a high frequency. It makes air vibrate backwards and forwards faster than a low-pitched sound which has a low frequency.

**Volume and amplitude**

Loud sounds make air vibrate backwards and forwards further than quieter sounds. They have a larger amplitude. Many sounds, such as a human voice, have very complex sound waves that have a mixture of frequencies and amplitudes.

## Analysing nerve impulses

The brain works out the pitch and volume of the sound being heard using the impulses generated by the hair cells in the cochlea. Higher-pitched sounds produce most hair cell movement near the oval window, lower-pitched sounds produce most movement further along the Organ of Corti. Loud sounds, such as the noise produced by cars, activate more hair cells than quieter sounds, such as those made by a bicycle.

## Direction of sound

The brain works out the direction sounds come from by comparing the impulses it gets from each ear. For example, if a sound is coming from the right, the right ear will hear it earlier and louder than the left ear.

**Cochlea**

*This is how the cochlea would appear if it could be unwound.*

**Organ of Corti**

**Oval window**

### Different sounds

*These boys know that vehicles are coming up from behind them on their right because their brains analyse the impulses produced by their ears.*

## HEARING AIDS

Many people cannot hear properly. Some are born deaf, others become deaf because of illness, old age or injury. Many deaf people hear with the help of hearing aids. These devices are incredibly small and can even fit inside the ear canal. They pick up sound waves and make them louder. Some types of hearing loss are caused because the hair cells in the cochlea have been damaged. Cochlear implants can help people who have this type of problem. These hearing aids directly stimulate the cochlea nerve.

### Cochlear implant

*Although cochlear implants like this one do not totally restore hearing, they do allow people to experience the sensation of sound.*

# A sense of position and movement
# is provided by the ears

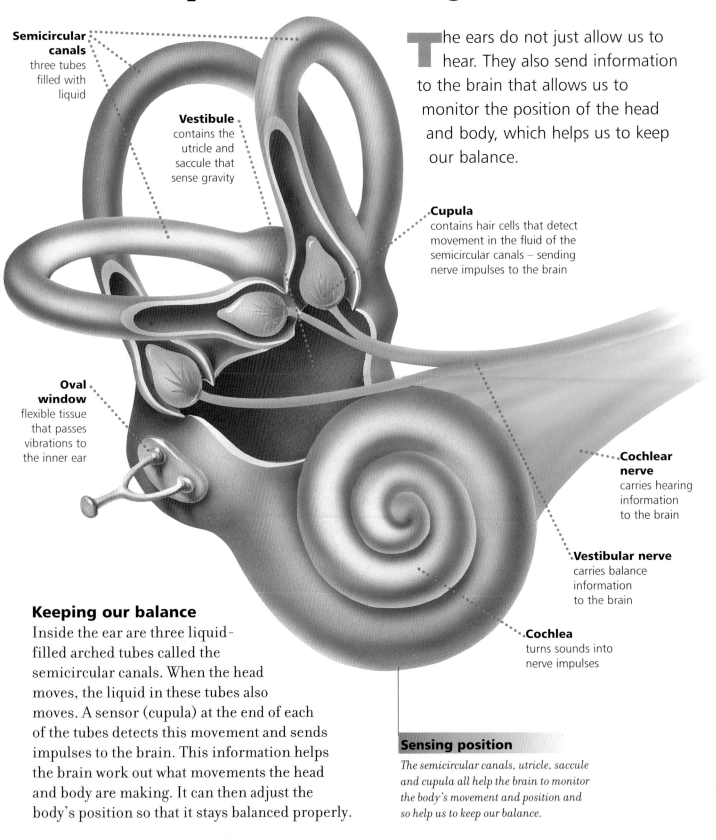

**Semicircular canals**
three tubes filled with liquid

**Vestibule**
contains the utricle and saccule that sense gravity

**Cupula**
contains hair cells that detect movement in the fluid of the semicircular canals – sending nerve impulses to the brain

**Oval window**
flexible tissue that passes vibrations to the inner ear

**Cochlear nerve**
carries hearing information to the brain

**Vestibular nerve**
carries balance information to the brain

**Cochlea**
turns sounds into nerve impulses

The ears do not just allow us to hear. They also send information to the brain that allows us to monitor the position of the head and body, which helps us to keep our balance.

## Keeping our balance

Inside the ear are three liquid-filled arched tubes called the semicircular canals. When the head moves, the liquid in these tubes also moves. A sensor (cupula) at the end of each of the tubes detects this movement and sends impulses to the brain. This information helps the brain work out what movements the head and body are making. It can then adjust the body's position so that it stays balanced properly.

### Sensing position

*The semicircular canals, utricle, saccule and cupula all help the brain to monitor the body's movement and position and so help us to keep our balance.*

## On the move?

The ear contains two other things that help the brain know which way up the body is and what movements it is making. In the space between the semicircular canals and the cochlea are areas called the utricle and saccule. These contain receptor hair cells covered with microscopic granules. When the head moves, these granules move and pull on the hairs which, in turn, send impulses to the brain.

## Not just the ears

The ears are not the only parts of the body that supply the brain with information about the position of the body. Eyes allow us to see where we are and what we are doing. There are also receptor cells in our muscles, joints and ligaments. They provide the brain with information about where all the different parts of the body are positioned and how they are moving. Without this information we would not be able to co-ordinate our movements or balance properly.

**Sensing movement**

*As this boy walks along, his brain is continually receiving information from his ears about the speed and direction of his movement.*

## MOTION SICKNESS

If you have ever felt sick on a boat, or when reading a book in a car, then you have experienced motion sickness. You get motion sickness because the information your brain receives from your eyes does not agree with the information it receives from the motion detectors in the ear.

The best thing to do is to try and look at the horizon – this way your brain will get the same message about what is happening to your body from both your eyes and your ears.

**Feeling green**

*Motion sickness occurs when the brain receives confusing information about movement.*

# The eyes convert light rays
# into nerve impulses

**M**ost people rely on sight more than any of the five senses. We use the pictures our eyes provide for everything, from moving about to remembering faces. In fact, more than two-thirds of the information the brain receives about the outside world comes from the eyes.

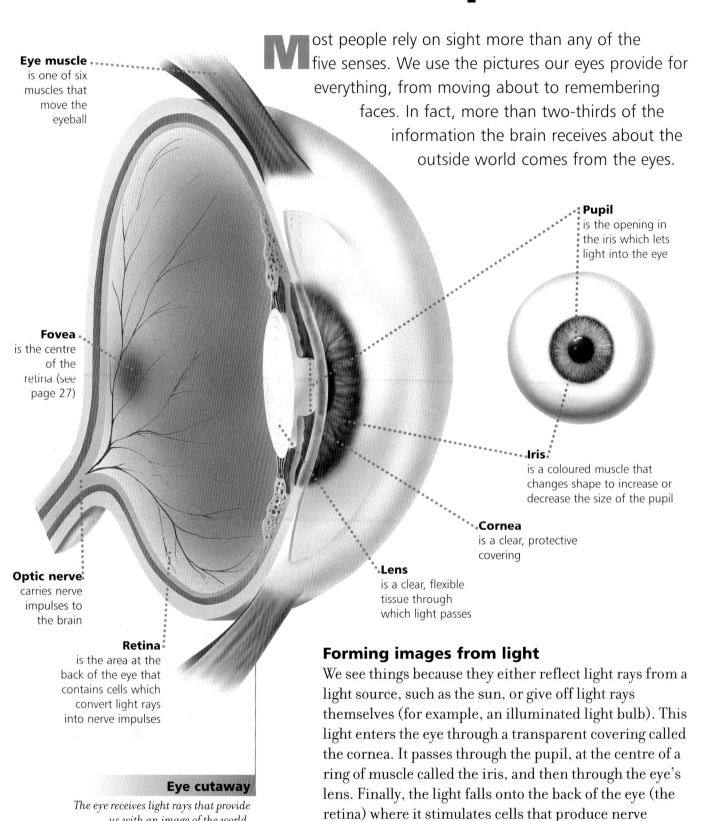

**Eye muscle**
is one of six muscles that move the eyeball

**Fovea**
is the centre of the retina (see page 27)

**Optic nerve**
carries nerve impulses to the brain

**Retina**
is the area at the back of the eye that contains cells which convert light rays into nerve impulses

**Pupil**
is the opening in the iris which lets light into the eye

**Iris**
is a coloured muscle that changes shape to increase or decrease the size of the pupil

**Cornea**
is a clear, protective covering

**Lens**
is a clear, flexible tissue through which light passes

**Eye cutaway**

*The eye receives light rays that provide us with an image of the world.*

## Forming images from light

We see things because they either reflect light rays from a light source, such as the sun, or give off light rays themselves (for example, an illuminated light bulb). This light enters the eye through a transparent covering called the cornea. It passes through the pupil, at the centre of a ring of muscle called the iris, and then through the eye's lens. Finally, the light falls onto the back of the eye (the retina) where it stimulates cells that produce nerve impulses that are sent to the brain (see pages 26–27).

## Focusing lens

We can see things clearly whether they are near or distant because the eye's lens can focus. Focusing makes the light rays entering the eye fall exactly onto the retina. Focusing happens automatically without us having to think about it. The eye's lens focuses because muscle around it makes it change shape.

## The power of the iris

The eye also allows us to see in different light conditions – from bright to dark – because of a ring of muscle called the iris. In bright light, the iris makes the pupil get smaller, protecting the retina from damage. In dark conditions, the iris makes the pupil get bigger to let in more light.

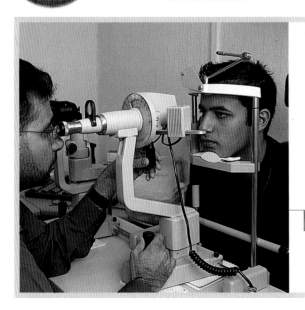

### Changing pupil size

*The iris makes the pupil larger (top) or smaller (bottom) to allow in more or less light. This allows us to see in different light conditions, although we cannot see as well in the dark as most animals.*

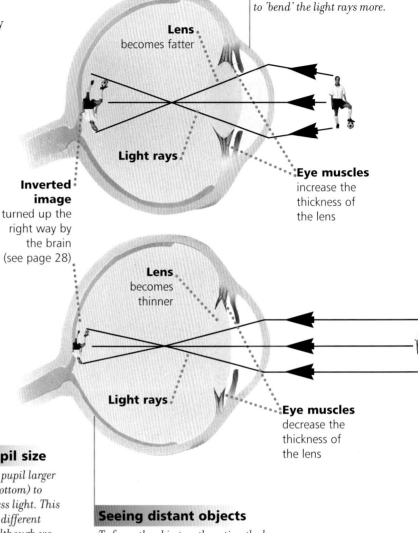

### Seeing near objects

*To focus the object on the retina the lens becomes fatter to 'bend' the light rays more.*

**Lens** becomes fatter

**Light rays**

**Inverted image** turned up the right way by the brain (see page 28)

**Eye muscles** increase the thickness of the lens

**Lens** becomes thinner

**Light rays**

**Eye muscles** decrease the thickness of the lens

### Seeing distant objects

*To focus the object on the retina the lens becomes thinner to 'bend' the light rays less. The cornea also helps the eye to focus light.*

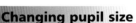

## EYESIGHT PROBLEMS

If you wear glasses then you know what happens if the eye does not focus properly – your vision goes fuzzy. Eyesight problems are normally caused because the eyeball is the wrong shape. If the eyeball is too long, then the eye's lens focuses images just in front of the retina. If the eyeball is too short then the opposite happens.

### Measuring the eyeball

*This patient is having the shape of his eyeball measured using a keratometer. It is important to have regular eye tests so that any eyesight problems can be detected early.*

# The eyes see
## colour and detail

The retina is the part of the eye that is stimulated by light rays. It produces nerve impulses that can be processed by the brain. The retina is covered with millions of cells that respond to light. These special cells are called rods and cones. Rods and cones do different jobs – rods allow us to see in dim light, while cones let us see colours when the light is good. Rods and cones contain special chemicals that change when light hits them. This process sets off the nerve impulses that travel along the optic nerve to the brain.

**Inside the eye**
*Here we can see the retina, where light is turned into nerve impulses that are sent to the brain via the optic nerve.*

**Lens**

**Fovea**
is packed with cones
(see opposite page)

**Optic nerve**

**Blind spot**
(see opposite page)

**Blood vessel**

**Retina**
contains rods and cones that are stimulated by light rays – producing nerve impulses that are sent to the brain

## Colour vision
There are three kinds of cone. Each one responds most strongly to one of three colours of light: blue, green or red. The brain can 'see' colours by analysing the impulses it gets from the cones. Some people have one (or more) type of cone missing or functioning poorly. This condition is called colour blindness. People who are colour blind cannot tell the difference between some colours, for example red and green.

## Seeing in dim light

Cones do not work well in dim light, which is why it becomes difficult to see colours as night falls. However, rods respond even in low levels of light. Rods do not give the brain any information about colours, but give an image of the world in shades of black and white.

## Seeing things clearly

Each eye has about 120 million rods and 6 million cones which are arranged on the retina in a special way. The centre of the retina (the fovea) is where the eye focuses the centre of any scene we look at. The fovea is jam-packed with cones – the rest of the retina is mainly full of rods. This means that the brain gets lots of detailed information about whatever is being studied most closely.

**Fovea**

*The fovea is a crater-like area at the centre of the retina. It is packed with cones that supply the brain with information about colour and detail.*

## THE BLIND SPOT

One area on the retina has no rods or cones. This blind spot is where the optic nerve and blood vessels enter the eye. It is quite easy to show that you have a blind spot. Pick up this book and hold it at arm's length from your face. Close your right eye and stare at the cross below. Now move the whole page towards you. When it gets about 12 cm from your face you should see that the circle next to it vanishes. This happens because the image of the circle falls on the blind spot.

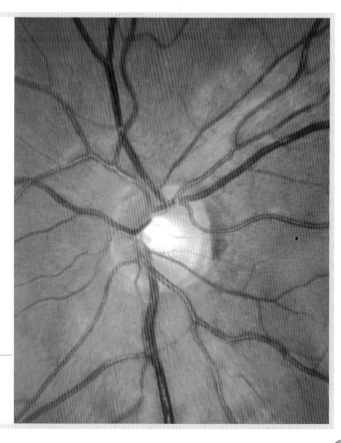

**Image of the retina**

*The pale area in the centre of the photograph shows where the optic nerve enters the eye. This is called the blind spot.*

# We use our brain to **understand what we see**

The eyes may collect visual information, but it is analysed by the brain – it is the brain that 'sees'. For example, the images focused on the retina are upside down. The brain takes the images and turns them the 'right' way round. Experiments have been done in which people wear glasses that make them see upside down. Their brains get used to this within just a few weeks.

## Learning to see

Sight is still not totally understood and scientists are still not completely sure how the brain 'knows' what it is seeing. However, it is clear that the brain uses its store of memories to interpret what it sees and work out what things are and, for example, how big they are. This process of recognition happens the instant we see something – faster than the blink of an eye!

### Image scanning

*The eye scans an image many times a second, moving from point to point as indicated by the red line above. This provides the brain with information so it can interpret what we see. For example, using our store of memories, we know this is a cat. We also know that, even though we cannot see them, it has four legs.*

## OPTICAL ILLUSIONS

The brain can often be tricked or confused by the visual information it gets from the eyes. For example, when you go to the cinema you see a series of still pictures. Because these are flashed up very quickly, the brain is tricked into seeing movement.

An optical illusion is an image that tricks the brain. For example, look at this cube – is it a picture of a cube with a bit missing, or is the front of the cube sticking out? The brain is confused because it is not provided with all the information it needs to work out what it is seeing.

## The big crossover

The visual impulses from the retina of each eye travel to the brain along the optic nerves. The optic nerves from each eye meet in the brain at a place called the optic chiasma. Here, the images from the right side of each eye go together to the visual cortex on the right side of the brain. Images from the left of each eye go together to the visual cortex in the left side of the brain.

### Visual pathway

*The nerve impulses from the eyes cross over at the optic chiasma. The brain combines images from the left and right eyes to produce a field of stereo vision.*

**Left field of vision**
this view is seen by the left eye only

**Field of stereo vision**
this view is seen by both eyes and has 'depth'

**Eyes**

**Optic nerves**
carry nerve impulses to the visual cortex

**Right field of vision**
this view is seen by the right eye only

**Optic chiasma**
is where the optic nerves meet

**Left visual cortex**

**Right visual cortex**

## Seeing depth

We get a slightly different view of the world from each eye. Try opening and closing each eye in turn to see this. The two different images from both eyes are combined into one view in the visual cortex at the back of the brain. This is called stereo vision. It has 'depth' and allows the brain to judge distances.

**29**

# Glossary

**Amplitude** The distance between the peak of a wave and its rest position. Waves carrying a lot of energy (eg. loud sound waves) have a large amplitude.

**Association neuron** Nerve cells that relay impulses from one neuron to another. Most are found in the brain and spinal cord.

**Braille** Special alphabet made up of raised dots, that enables the blind to read using their finger tips.

**Cerebral cortex** The surface layer of the cerebrum (the largest part of the brain). The area of the brain where information from the sense organs is processed.

**Cochlea** A complex structure in the inner ear, shaped like a shell, where sound vibrations are converted into electrical nerve impulses, which are sent to the brain.

**Cone** A type of cell in the retina of the eye that responds to bright, coloured light.

**Cornea** A transparent layer at the front of the eye. It helps the eye lens focus rays of light.

**Eardrum** A thin membrane that lies at the end of the ear canal and separates the outer ear from the middle ear. The eardrum vibrates when sound waves hit it.

**Fovea** The area of the retina which has the highest concentration of cone cells. The area on which the centre of any view is focused.

**Frequency** The number of waves made in one second.

**Hypothalamus** A part of the brain that monitors and regulates body functions such as hunger, thirst and temperature.

**Iris** A coloured ring of muscle that surrounds the pupil. The size of the iris can change to allow more or less light into the eye.

**Lens** The clear, flexible tissue that sits near the front of the eye. The shape of the lens can be changed to focus light onto the retina.

**Motor neuron** A nerve cell that carries nerve impulses from the brain and spinal cord to muscles.

**Nerve** A bundle of nerve cells.

**Nerve impulse** An electrical signal that travels along a neuron. Nerve impulses carry information to, from and within the central nervous system and brain.

**Neuron** A nerve cell that carries nerve impulses. There are billions of neurons in the body.

**Olfactory bulb** Nerve fibres carrying nerve impulses from smell receptors in the nose meet in this structure that lies just above the nasal cavity.

**Optic chiasma** Part of the brain where the nerves from the left and right eye meet.

**Organ of Corti** Part of the cochlea containing hair-like receptor cells that respond to sound vibrations and send nerve impulses to the brain.

**Pupil** The opening at the front of the eye surrounded by the iris.

**Receptor cells** Special cells that respond to different stimuli and cause a nerve impulse to be sent along a neuron.

**Retina** The layer at the back of the eye that contains rod and cone receptor cells.

**Rod** A type of light-sensitive cell mainly found around the sides of the retina. Rods send nerve impulses to the brain that let us see in black and white when light conditions are poor.

**Semicircular canals** Three liquid-filled arched tubes in the inner ear.

**Sensory neuron** A nerve cell that carries nerve impulses from sensory receptors to the brain and spinal cord.

**Spinal cord** The tube of nervous tissue that runs from the brain down the backbone. Many nerves link the spinal cord to the rest of the body.

**Stimuli** The things – light, smell, tastes, sound and touch – that make the sense organs send nerve impulses to the spinal cord and brain.

**Taste bud** Receptor cells found on the papillae of the tongue that respond to taste chemicals found in food.

**Utricle and saccule** Small structures in the inner ear that send the brain information about the position of the head and the direction of movement.

# Find out more

These are just some of the websites where you can find out more information about our senses. Many of the websites also provide information and illustrations about other systems and processes of the human body.

**www.bbc.co.uk/health/kids**
A website specifically designed for kids – featuring information on body and health matters. Look at parts of the body, including the eyes and ears, in more detail.

**www.howstuffworks.com**
Go to the 'science stuff' section of this site for loads of information on the five senses.

**www.ich.ucl.ac.uk/kidsandteens/index.html**
Visit this website of the world-famous Great Ormond Street Hospital for Children to find out lots about how doctors can help make us better. You'll find a great 'body tour' and you can even email in questions.

**www.hhmi.org/senses**
In-depth articles on seeing, hearing and smelling the world.

**www.ajkids.com**
The best search engine for asking questions about science – just type in your query, press 'enter' and you'll be shown where to get the best answer.

**www.brainpop.com/health**
Find out all about the parts of the body, including the five senses. You can even download animated movies which will show you how they work.

**www.kidshealth.org**
Find lots of information on this website about all the different parts of the body – including the sense organs – and how to keep them healthy.

**www.bbc.co.uk/science/humanbody**
Another site devoted to the parts of the body and how they work – put your senses to the 'sense test' to see if they are being tricked.

**www.nationalgeographic.com/ngkids/0006/senses/senses1.html**
Find out loads about the super senses of animals – big and small, friendly and scary.

**www.vision3d.com**
A website that features 3-dimensional illusions that trick your eyes. Includes a section on visual health.

**www.abc.net.au/science**
The Lab – an Australian website that has lots of features and up-to-date news items about different science subjects, including the five senses.

# Index

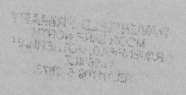